BRAIN HUG MEDITATION

Short Stories, Poetry & Exercises
For Meditation

KaZ Akers

Dedication

This is for every teacher who teachers some form of meditation,

and every student who practices some form of meditation.

Dedicating our lives to mental and physical health.

Which, in my book, is all health.

Acknowledgements

I wish to thank every teacher I've ever had, the teachers I resonated with and those that I didn't.

I learned from all of them.

My teachers weren't perfect and neither am I. That's the beauty of it.

Any teacher that claims to be perfect is not only kidding us but also kidding themselves.

Living as a human is a flawed and fantastic existence.

No one is 100% in all aspects of their lives. That's what I really love about being a continuing student.

I love discovering new teachers all the time.

Some I've outgrown. Some I've stuck with for a long time.

I've walked away from teachers I was convinced (by myself and them) had all the answers. They didn't. Neither do I.

Teachers will come and go and students will come and go.

All I've ever asked of my teachers was honestly, transparency, and genuineness.

I expect that of myself, too, and when I'm struggling I go right back into the classroom.

Life is learning.

I appreciate every student I've ever taught, and every student who has taught me, which happens in every class.

My eternal gratitude to JAB CREATIVE - Jack Akers-Brownlee - who designed my cover and the symbol inside. He also happens to be my very talented son. I'm grateful to him and for him every.single.day.

I'm so grateful for my husband, Todd, who supports my writing and my teaching, even when it isn't easy.

And to my publisher, without whom you would not be reading this!

KaZ

Introduction

The meditations within this book are based on breath meditation and Qigong meditation.

Qigong is a moving meditation. It's the mother of Tai Chi, which is a martial art.

Sometimes we can't just sit there, we have to move.

At least that's how I feel.

"Shut up and sit down" hasn't always worked for me.

I found through Qigong movement I'm able to work things out with myself in a more active way.

Even Zen meditation includes walking meditation.

Some days I know sitting is exactly what I need. Other days I have to move.

You'll find active and more passive exercises, short stories and poems for contemplation and meditation between the pages of this book.

Sometimes the activity is just working with your breath.

Your breath IS constantly moving throughout the day whether you are aware of it or not. The contents of this book may help you to be more aware.

Forget about releasing or stopping your thoughts. These short stories, poems and exercises will naturally take care of that without any struggle.

You'll realize there are times when you effortlessly stop actively thinking about anything in particular; except perhaps "breathe in, breathe out".

The short stories that exemplify releasing, relaxing, accepting and honoring yourself and others. (I use the word accept instead of tolerate. Not my favorite word. Would you prefer I accept you or tolerate you?)

I came to meditation 32 years ago because my life was a bit of a mess; a relationship mess.   I'm grateful I was in that mess and to the person who shared that mess with me. Otherwise, I may not have found meditation when I did, and it may not be playing the significant, life-changing, role it now plays.

I'm also grateful to Monty Python, and lyricist Eric Idle, for their eternal ear worm "Always look on the bright side of life." When it isn't driving me crazy, it's giving me a boost. No matter how bleak things may look there's always a way to look at things from a different perspective.

With love…KaZ

Preface

I wanted to make every page in this book blank except for the dedication, acknowledgements, introduction and chapter page.

The reason being: meditation is different for every individual. We try it on and see what fits. Or throw the spaghetti against the wall and see what sticks. (That's what I learned in the Italian neighborhood where I grew up. Now I'm sure there's a gadget or hack for that.)

What I AM going to do is leave a few pages blank at the end of the book for your own notes.

Or for you to design your own meditation practice. Most likely, it will change year to year. (YEAR? You ask. Yes, I have faith in you.)

You can write down dates so you can refer back to your note pages and see how you've progressed, regressed (yes, I've done that myself), changed, morphed and grown.

That is what meditation is all about. GROWTH.

What works for you today may not work next month or next year. I'm certainly living proof that what I've experienced, and what has "stuck", looks very different from where I began.

Make up your own meditations.

Teach other people what you've learned.

This is a **"pay it forward"** kind of practice.

You may never become a certified master teacher, but you can be someone's guide.

What I have included here are my favorite meditations and some stories and poems to meditate on.

I admit I'm not your usual teacher. My ideas on meditation are not what is "popular", or what the more celebrated teachers teach. It's what I've learned in 32 years of practice and study and 22 years of teaching.

Take what works, leave what doesn't.

Change exercises to work better for you if need be.

This is all about YOU!

If you don't like the word "meditation", don't use it.

If you don't like the word "mindfulness" (I don't), don't use it either.

Call this practice "Paddling Down The Mississippi" for all I care.

Just make an attempt.

Give yourself a few minutes every day to care for yourself and paddle down the Mississippi.

The scenery is AMAZING.

Contents

Once You're Done

Once you are done with this book if you decide not to keep it in your library I ask that you share it with a friend, colleague or even a stranger.

Other options are to donate it to a library, prison reading program, poetry group or any organization you feel may benefit from this book.

Please do not throw it away, or recycle it, so it doesn't end up in our environment.

Thank you,

KaZ

Before You Read

This book can be read in or out of sequence. There is no wrong or right way to read it.

Before you turn a page, before you read a short story, poem or exercise, before you do anything….

BREATHE.

Take a moment, if you are comfortable, to close your eyes fully, close them partially or keep them open and put your attention on a focal point.

Take a breath in through your nose and out through your nose. Breathe easily, not too shallow and not too deeply - just fully - in through your nose and out of your nose.

Purposefully.

Calmly.

Effortlessly and gently.

With no goal, agenda or intention.

Just breathe.

And if it moves you, take in a big breath in through your nose and out through your nose.

Let it fill your lungs slowly.

Let it expand your diaphragm.

Take your time.

No need to hurry.

Hurry can wait until later.

Fill your lungs with oxygen.

Slow down your mind, your your body, and your movements.

Release slowly and begin…

Hopefully, this will put you in a receptive frame of mind to get the most out of each page you read.

Let the words speak to you the way they speak to YOU!

I'm unattached to you "getting" what I meant when I wrote these short stories, poems and exercises.

However, my purpose is that you approach this book to help yourself to achieve a meditative state.

You may open the pages one day and not be feeling your best.

You may open the pages another day and want to enhance an already positive feeling.

Regardless, the book will guide you to where you need to be.

Just keep breathing.

Be aware if your breaths are shallow or forced.

If something "hits" you, breathe through it.

Laugh, cry, burp, fart while you are reading this book.

It's all a part of the total experience.

I think I did all of that while I was writing it. (My truth be told.)

This book is intended to enhance your health emotionally, mentally, psychologically, physically and whatever you consider to be spiritually.

If a part of it "hits you the wrong way" then that is an opportune time to explore the cause of that discomfort or dislike.

Release any need to accomplish anything while reading this book.

What happens for you, happens.

Written with love and compassion plain and simple.

KaZ

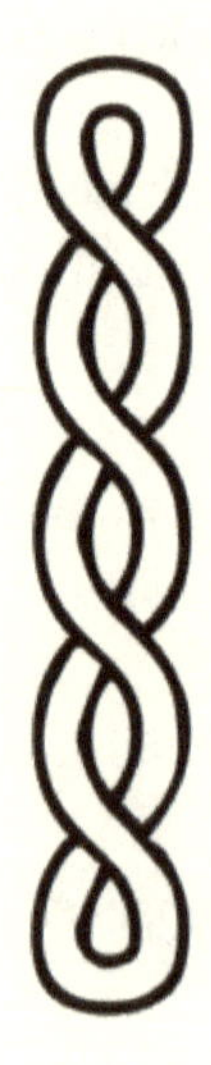

The Symbol

The symbol is an elongated circle, but it is twisted.

It has no beginning and no end.

It represents our lives: an unending series of twists, turns and curves.

Some of those curves travel over others and some travel under others. It is all in how you look at them.

It is smooth at the curve points to represent that even the twists and turns in our lives don't need to sharp edged or abrupt.

Your perspective and perception is exactly your perspective and perception.

It was specifically designed to use as a focal point for meditation, contemplation or just to observe.

Here Is The Secret To Starting And Maintaining A Home Meditation Practice.

It's not REALLY a secret.

These are three questions I get asked all the time by my students:

"How do I keep my home meditation practice going?"

"How do I START a home meditation practice?"

"Why am I able to do fine in meditation class but when I try to do it at home my practice just falls apart?"

These questions have a common theme.

Here are some answers that work for me. I'll bet they work for you, too. If not, try something else. There is plenty of information out there.

The blanket answer is "you're trying too hard.

My motto is: "if you're breathing, you can meditate".

You're putting so much pressure on yourself to meditate at a certain time of the day, for a certain amount of time, and in a certain way.

What I've discovered over the years is that meditation is more and easier than you may think.

Do your best to designate a place for meditation.

If you think about it your entire home is an opportunity to meditate. Try the sofa, the lounge chair, the chaise outside on the patio, a soft patch of grass in your yard, in a park, or anywhere you can put a blanket or cushion.

I've sat on carpeted stairs, and on the porch stoop. I've meditated, with my eyes open, on the New York City subway!

"How long do I need to meditate?" comes with some added pressure.

I say as long as you CAN meditate.

I'm the last person to ever tell you if you don't meditate for X amount of time, or more, that it's fruitless or you might as well not bother.

If ANYONE tells you that, kindly excuse yourself.

I went to a 4-day silent meditation retreat run by a very well known organization. The silent part was wonderful. Eating outdoors in silence, staying silent in the residence, and meditating in silence was a gift.

What I couldn't wrap my mind around was that I was instructed to meditate in one way and one way only. I was instructed that this was the only correct way to meditate.

It didn't feel right then and it doesn't feel right now.

I certainly don't instruct my students, or teachers I train, that it's my way or the highway.

Needless to say, I made the best of that retreat but I've never returned.

Meditation looks and feels many, many different ways.

It's almost like each individual needs their own prescription for meditation.

How do I know this?

Through trial and error as a practitioner, student and as a teacher. I see what works for a broad cross-section of students over and over again.

I've been meditating for decades and in many instances I've gotten as much out of a 5-minute meditation as a two-hour meditation.

To answer the first question:

"How do I keep my home practice going?"

Do you like how good you feel during a meditation, yoga, Qigong or Tai Chi class?

Grab that good feeling, take what you've learned in class, or online, and plunk yourself down in a chair, on a mat or in the grass. Or do Qigong moving meditation. Release pressuring yourself to replicate the circumstances or feelings in a class or in any one meditation session.

If you have a semi-regular practice at home, that's great. If possible, find other times to do it outside of what you already are accomplishing.

Once something becomes a habit - and it takes about 21 days to form a habit - your mind and body will crave it. That goes for good and not-so-good habits.

I'll tack my meditation sessions onto the end of my workouts. I'll meditate in between chapters of a book I am reading (like this one). If I'm having my tea on the patio, it is SO easy to float right into a meditation because the surroundings are more conducive to tranquility.

Binge-watching or streaming show? Close your eyes and do deep breathing between episodes!

Of course, it would be optimum if you carved out time to sit in meditation and formally meditate.

Choose a quiet room without much noise or traffic.

Pick a chair that you like, one that is comfortable enough to sit in for a while. I guarantee the next thing you know you'll have been sitting for 30 minutes.

Chanting and mantra is great at the beginning of a meditation journey. It helps keep you present and engaged. You can't actively thinking while repeating the words.

Listening to meditative music.

Do you want to light a candle? DO IT!

Incense? Why not?

Set the mood.

When you set the mood, and make yourself a space, it will have more meaning for you. It puts you in the meditative frame of mind.

Find somewhere you may have some uninterrupted time.

Meditation is one of those practices you must do continuously to accumulate more lasting benefits. Regardless, if you're only are able to find time a few times a week to do it, that far outweighs not doing it at all.

Question number 2:

"How do I start a home practice?"

This is totally up to you.

But STARTING is 50% of DOING home meditation.

TODAY'S THE DAY!

Do some research, take some classes.

Try things on and see what fits.

Bring them ALL home.

After that, experiment with different types of meditations, in different locations in your home or outdoors, for different amounts of time

You may also do one technique for a while and then try something new.

The point is TRY IT and try it long enough to see what works for you.

Don't just meditate once for 5 minutes, say "this isn't working, I still have thoughts and I'm not getting any more peaceful" and then quit.

That's not meditating.

That is letting your brain dictate to you:

"I'm bored."

"I'm tired."

"What am I making for dinner?"

"Did I pay that bill?"

"Did I make the kids lunch?'

"Did I feed the dog (cat, fish, bird, hamster, llama?)"

…and on and on and on.

That's the brain fighting you to make it more peaceful.

Your brain is used to go, go, go. It even gets used to chaos.

That means you need to retrain your brain.

When your brain and mind is more peaceful then your body will

be more peaceful, too.
Meditating at the very least is being in the moment and focusing on something:

A mantra, a chant, a quote, a candle, water flowing, birds flying, petting your dog, music, the wind blowing, deep breathing, and YES, even silence.
It's pretty limitless, depending on your openness.
Let your brain get used to being relieved of the watch for a few moments. You'll continue to have thoughts, but let go of actively THINKING for a while.
It's a thought, BIG DEAL. It will be there when you're done. If not, most likely it will return. Or perhaps it wasn't all that important.
Find opportunities during your day to get into a meditative state.
Snippets of time will turn into moments and then minutes and the next thing you know you'll be in that state of mind for longer and longer periods.
Last, but certainly not least, here's my answer to question number 3:
"Why am I able to do fine in meditation class but when I try to do it at home my practice just stalls?"
Time, commitments, family, work, illness, vacations - YOU NAME IT - interfere with us bringing home what we did in class.
Here is where the three questions overlap.
Take the time, make the time, schedule it, carve it out…
How much do you need it?
You may have no challenges, too, and meditation can enhance your life.
If you're asking yourself any of these questions, I imagine that you need it.
It's not hard to sit in a class and follow what a teacher instructs.
What IS hard is to make meditation, in its many forms, a priority along with brushing your teeth, doing the laundry, preparing

meals, etc.

Your mental, emotional, physical, psychological and (if it applies to you) spiritual health is just as important as anything else in your life. Jump right in.

NOW is a good time.

Look For The Adventure.

When life appears upside down,
look for the adventure.
When things do not show up as you wish,
look for the point of the experience.
When your anticipation
does not elicit the outcome you wish,
examine the outcome.
It may be better than expected.
Or surprisingly different.
In a good way.
Shades of red appear in the blue.
Shades of orange appear in the red.
Sun is always behind the clouds.
Always.

Two Tubes of Lipstick And A Gallon Of Vodka.

I'm sure you can't tell from the title of this short story that it's an end of life story.

The poignant thing is that THIS part of the story is really wonderfully funny.

At least I think so.

You can judge for yourself.

Here goes:

I originally wrote this when my family member was near the end of her life. She passed away only a few days after I finished writing it.

NOW, More than being an anecdote, this story is a tribute to her, because she was the proverbial spit-fire…

The somber note is that Alzheimer's slowly altered her memory, and her behavior and shortened her life.

For ANYONE out there with a family member or a friend suffering from Alzheimer's, my heart goes out to you. Educate yourself. Be patient and loving with YOURSELF AND your loved one. Times like these show us what we're made of.

For both privacy and ease of writing I'm going to refer to her as Ms. T.

Ms. T. lived a wonderful life full of family, friends, events, travel, parties, rubbing elbows with notables, golf games and real estate. She was a whiz at selling real estate and she was a great golfer. She played with some heavy hitters. (Pardon the pun,) In her prime, real estate and golf went together extremely well. I imagine they still go together today - BIG deals being made on the 9th hole.

To the very end, in her late 80's, she was a classy woman -

always well-dressed, always putting her best foot forward.
She had a closet that every woman with taste and style wanted to raid…
…and a smile that lit up a room. A big, broad smile.
Ms. T. wore a specific color of Revlon lipstick. Revlon, not L'Oreal, or MAC or Urban Decay, but Revlon.
One day she noticed she was running out of her lipstick and asked her daughter to pick up another tube.
I'll also add that Ms. T. had a taste for good vodka. She loved her evening cocktail hour. Who can begrudge an 87 year-old woman her cocktail hour?
In addition to her favorite lipstick, she also requested her favorite vodka in the convenient gallon economy size.
Her daughter, being the loving daughter she is, bought her mother TWO tubes of lipstick.
Those who wear lipstick we all know how this goes - eventually every cosmetic company stops making our favorite shade of lipstick and we have to find a new color that never quite matches or looks as good as the old color.
Two tubes is an assurance of continuing to have the right color.
The vodka, well, if you drink vodka you know what works.
(I personally don't drink vodka because it makes me mean. I don't really drink much at all. I can't hold my liquor now. I can hear a friend, whom I've known since college, saying: "you never could drink", although I field tested it. It was college, what can I say?)
Later in the day loving daughter delivered the two tubes of lipstick and the gallon of vodka.
Not being ungrateful, Ms. T. asked why she bought her two tubes of lipstick.
In her daughter's mind it was for the aforementioned reasons.
They certainly make sense to me.
Ms. T. said she may not live long enough to finish the two tubes of lipstick.

"Then why did I get you such a big bottle of vodka if you think you might not be around much longer?"
"Oh, I'll be around long enough to drink the vodka!"
(Appropriate drum splash.
That reminds me of a quote from The Godfather:
"Leave the gun, take the cannoli!"
"Forget the lipstick, get the vodka!"

*If you, a family member or friend are struggling with Alzheimer's contact: www.alz.org

Focal Point Meditation.

There are wonderful meditation focal points to be found everywhere.

Here I have given you a photo of one of my favorites..

I have found myself not staring, but focusing on it on many occasions.

It can induce a peaceful feeling.

It appears to go on and on.

Sometimes it will ripple or wave in my eyes.

Take some time to look at this photo and allow your eyes to relax while looking.

Breathe easily and effortlessly in through your nose and out through your nose.

Blink when necessary.

Friendship

I've moved quite a few times.
I've met a lot of people. Many marvelous people.
I've made short term, for the moment or situation, long term and
life long friends.
Friends spread throughout the world.
It's heartbreaking when you find out that one of those beautiful
people has a terminal
illness.
I just found out that my friend is in hospice. I wondered why I
hadn't heard from her in
a while.
My first reaction was tears.
Then ANGER. (But anger does me no good. Who am I going to
blame?)
Later Sorrow.
And now?
JOY!
Joy because I know her. Joy because she is in my life.
AND
Joy because when she is gone she leaves an INDELIBLE
impression on my heart.
How many people can we say that about?
For me, quite a few.
They know who they are.
They are literally all over the world

I have very little family left in the world.
I started off with a really small family to begin
with and now these friends ARE my family.

Just to make sure there is no misunderstanding, my friends:
I love you.
I love each and every one of you.
I do my best to say it as often as I can in person, by email, text, etc.
If there is a mode of communication to use, I'm going to use it.
Does it scare me to express my love?
Absolutely not.
Not everyone can express it as openly as I do, and that's ok.
I have friends who, culturally, it's not in their nature to hug and
express verbal love.
But they do with me.

My mother used to chastise me when I was a child because she
said I never met a
person I didn't like. Although these days I do my best to be open
AND cautious.

My friend is a kind, caring, generous, funny, and compassionate
person.
Why her?
So many questions and most, I know, will never be answered.
Sometimes answers are really overrated.
Does she know how much I treasure her friendship?
In this fickle world of here today, gone tomorrow friends, this
friendship stuck, even
when I moved thousands of miles away from her.

She vacationed in the town where I moved. I got to see her
every year. We would have lunch, breakfast.She always insisted
on paying. I tried every time. I'll add generous the long list of
her attributes. Sometimes she would make me a scrumptious
meal at her place.

The last time I saw her she had mutual friends over for dinner. It

was a wonderful night.
Whenever I was in town we did our best, given our schedules, to see each other.
We became even better friends once I moved than we were when we lived in the same
town.
It's funny how that works.
Some friends simply fade away when you aren't in close proximity.
Life has a way of moving forward and, despite our best efforts, friendships just fade.
It doesn't mean you are loved any less or you love any less.
When you least expect it, there are some friends who make an effort to stay in
touch.

Her illness and rapid decline have left me in shock.
That is NOT what she would want.
I stayed awake most of last night thinking about her. About us.
She would want me to CELEBRATE her!
Lift a glass of her favorite Prosecco to her.
Name an outfit after her.
She would want me to dance the day she leaves on her continuing journey.
So...I will.
Although I know she cannot see or speak due to her advancing illness, still, I wrote her
an email.
An email she'll never read.
I did it anyway.
It's the best way for me to say "bon voyage."

Tell them NOW how you feel.
Without fear.

Give them a generous hug.
Who cares who hears or sees it?

My friend would not want me to be kept awake at night grieving
for her. "You need
your beauty sleep." Then she would laugh this raucous laugh.
She would tell me to live my best life. To be the ambassador of
my own happiness.
To celebrate every precious day and NOT to forget how pre-
cious every day is.
She loved to travel so I will continue to travel carrying her with
me in my heart - seeing
it through her eyes.
I won't say I miss you.
I know by just thinking about you that you are always here with
me.

*Update:
After I wrote this I was on the phone with her best friend. We
were talking about
our relationship with her.
Immediately after she hung up with me she got the call that our
friend had passed away 10
minutes before…
while we were talking about her.
So....
...guess what I did?

I danced.

Dreams

Dreams,
our supreme lifeline.
Small dreams.
Big dreams.
Everything dream in between.
Dreams appear as
thunder and lightening.
As a rhythmic clock ticking.
They follow us… whispering.
Dreams stand in front of us to
bellow, prod, and bluster.
Asking.
Begging.
Pleading.
Cajoling.
Beseeching us to listen.
They are realized.
Rejected.
Rejuvenated.
Forgotten and fragmented.
Dreams show us who we are,
who we wish to be,
who we are not.
Dreams cannot be stolen from us.
They ARE us.
Where we go,
what we do,
we are the dream.
So dream.

Here's Another Simple But Effective Meditation Exercise.

*Read through this meditation before trying it.

Sit in a comfortable position in a comfortable place.

You may close your eyes, leave them open or leave them partially open.

If you wish to leave them partially or fully open find and a stable focal point.

Place your hands together and rub them together.

Keep rubbing your hands together, rub them up and down, rub them side to side, focus on the length of your fingers, and focus on your palms.

Rub them in circle clockwise, and then rub them anti-clockwise in a circle.

Just keep rubbing them while you feel them heating up and getting warm.

Feel all the parts of your palms getting warm.

When you reach that feeling of being nice and warm, clap your hands together.

Clap them tilted so they focus on the palms, and clap along your fingers.

Keep clapping.

Let your hands clap in a semi circle either way, and keep clapping.

Now rub them together one more time.

Rub, rub, rub.

You should feel more heat.

Rub, rub, rub, rub, rub, rub.

Finish by placing them palms up on your legs, or your lap.

What you most likely will feel is some sort of tingling, vibration or pulsing.

As you breathe easily and effortlessly in through your nose, and out through your nose, just sit and allow your focus to be on your hands for a few moments.

Continue to breathe in and out of your nose

When you stop feeling any sensations in your hands, you may open your eyes, or release the meditation.

Now, wasn't that nice!

My One Year Commitment To Silence: The Aftermath.

Is it possible to be silent in a noisy world?

It was quite the year!

I learned so much about myself, those around me, strangers and life.

To say the least, my one year commitment to speaking as little as possible morphed.

It morphed, in general, for good reasons.

Not to speak in a noisy, chattery, speaking world is tough. I kid you not.

The impact it had on family and friends speaks volumes about them and me.

Oddly enough, for the most part, it was accepted by strangers. That was a bit shocking. I wasn't speaking and some assumed I didn't or couldn't speak.

Any companion who was with me at the time would explain, if it felt necessary.

I'd get two thumbs up, shrugs, sideways glances and " wow, that is SO cool!"

I was only silent on Sundays. What I called "Silent Sunday". As a day-to-day practice it's very difficult. I can't separate myself from my family, friends, colleagues and the extended world for long periods of time. That type of practice I had to leave to formal silent retreats. So I opted for once day a week of silence. No matter what.

Silence in meditation is no problem for me. It's a welcome practice for this Chatty Cathy. I've been participating in silent meditation for years.

What prompted me to take on this year long practice?

My reasoning for 52 days of silence was to be a better listener. To truly HEAR what others, and the world (including nature) are saying.

Why Sunday?

It seemed to be the best day where there's not a lot to do, not too many interactions, and the end or beginning of each week - depending on how you look at it.

BUT add travel, visiting family and friends and you have a REAL challenge.

I like a challenge.

Not everyone around me embraced my little " experiment."

It frustrated some, especially those who are challenged with charades. I'll admit I made some hand and facial gestures and wrote some things down.

I wasn't speaking, it didn't mean I wasn't communicating at all.

Can you imagine spending every Sunday staring blankly at people, but moreover, having them stare back blankly at you?

I live in the world, not in some secluded retreat away from any interactions or distractions. Because of that it felt extremely challenging to embark on this journey.

More times than I can count when a stranger discovered my practice they were surprisingly supportive and remarked that they needed to do something similar. Who doesn't want more peace and quiet?

Needing to do it and actually doing it is a whole other matter altogether. I was walking, (but not talking), living, breathing proof of that.

Friends who really know me took it in stride. "Ok, we won't talk or video chat on Sunday."

Family was a mixed bag. My son was immediately on board.

Other members of the family, well, not so much.

Either they said it made no sense to them or it made them feel uncomfortable.

One person actually insulted me asking how could I do that to my son? They actually said this in front of my son. My wise, old soul son was quick to respond that he was used to it and it didn't bother him at all. Plus, I'd think it gave him a day's reprieve from my yacking.

Some family members would get testy and tell me just to talk. I wouldn't. It wasn't my issue that they were uncomfortable with it. If I did speak, I felt defeated, or that I was failing in a promise I made to myself.

Some tried to catch me making any sound at all. "Ah, ha! I HEARD YOU!" They would say that they heard me breathe or snicker or blow my nose. Basically challenging me that I was faking or I couldn't do it. Yes, I know, again, that wasn't about me.

All in all, in the long run, everyone eventually came around.

I believe it was because of my steadfast commitment. Regardless.

I made up my rules as I went along, always with the intent of LISTENING!

What did I do on Silent Sunday?

Read, write, play percussion instruments, meditate (of course), do Qigong, workout, walk, study, watch a movie, take a long car ride - anything that didn't involve me speaking.

What did I learn?

I learned that somedays you just need to shut up!

Sorry, blunt, but there it is.

What I hear and observe in a day of silence is more than in a week of talking.

The sun is brighter, the flowers are more fragrant, others' words are more meaningful and powerful.

You hear things that people knowingly and unknowingly reveal about themselves and their life.

In some cases they give themselves away: their true nature, true feelings, idiosyncrasies, doubts, strengths, fears and flaws. If I'm aren't speaking I'm not hearing either, right?

I would watch a person as much as I would listen to them..

I discovered a picture really IS worth a thousand words.

Often my face, and your face, says a lot more about how we are feeling, and what we are up to, than our words.

Have you really LOOKED at things lately?

We talk to mask our feelings. We fill the air with chatter, so we don't have to be in our heads.

We can get out of our heads AND be quiet.

"Sure, KaZ, how?" I've met a lot of "PROVE IT! people. I'm happy to take on that challenge.

It's easy! JUST TRY IT.

This "ain't" about your mamma, your spouse, partner, friends, colleagues or your neighbor.

This is about you and peace of mind.

It is about you and awareness.

It's about you and understanding the bigger picture. The picture beyond your sometimes insular world.

We stop walking away from an encounter asking: "What did they say?" "Did I answer that question?" We don't get to a destination and ask: "How did I get here? I don't remember that trip."

So now what?

I'm back to speaking on Sundays.

I miss it.

I loved it.

I loved sitting peacefully with another person in the same room, or the same house, and we didn't feel the pressure or need to talk.

I loved the release of pressure to verbally communicate anytime, anywhere. Plus, it got easier for me as time went on.

Have I considered doing it again?

Without a doubt. It is now an integrated part of me.

I'd like to add a silent weekend here and there and see if I can accomplish one silent week a year.

I'd love to have others join me and share their experiences.

Silence **IS** golden.

Mind is Muse.

The silence creeps up on me like thick mist.
 I want no part of it.
My mind races with deliberate dialogue.
 "This is for your own good."
THEN
It implores,
continually ignoring it's own pleas.
Instructed to strive for "no mind".
Devoid of thoughts, mind fights it's own neurotic battle.
Looking through broken glass, the heart lacerates another useless
tirade.
"You are human,
"you think."
THAT is what makes you human.
Allow thoughts.
Release thinking.
That is the gift.
Struggle is optional.
Make peace with your mind.
Make peace with your thoughts.
Are you listening?
Mind is not master.
Mind is collaborator.
Mind is muse.

The Easiest, Most Effective Meditation, That Doesn't Feel Like Meditation At All.

This is one of the easiest, most effective meditation exercises I've ever taught. I've had a 95% success rate teaching it to students in the moment. The other 5% have come back in the future and told me it worked for them when they were on their own without any distractions.

It's simple, but really powerful. That's the feedback. I'm not making it up.
Get ready to breathe and focus for just a few minutes.
If for some reason you don't have success immediately, don't worry, it's totally ok! Just try again at another time.

Read through the exercise once before trying it.

Sit in a comfortable place, in a comfortable position.
The first few times you try this please don't lie down.
Lying down signals to the brain to sleep. It will feel good to fall asleep but you won't benefit from the exercise.

If you're comfortable, close your eyes. If you aren't comfortable closing your eyes you may leave them half open or open focused on an object.

Start by gently, easily and effortlessly breathing in and out through your nose.
Allow your chest and abdomen to expand naturally.
Do that for a few moments just focusing on your breathing.

When you feel at peace with just breathing in and out of your nose, draw your attention to your heart beat.
Feel for your heartbeat.
Take your time and don't pressure yourself if it takes a few moments.

Keep breathing and feeling for your heartbeat.

When you feel it open your eyes and conclude the meditation.

YES! This is the mediation.

If meditation is difficult for you, guess what? YOU JUST MEDITATED.

Plus, I'd be willing to bet the only things you were thinking about were your breath and your heartbeat.

If you could not feel your heartbeat, as I said in the beginning don't worry about it. Just try it again another time.

Pass it on by teaching others this easy meditation. They'll be grateful I am sure because it is so easy.

It's meditating that doesn't feel like meditation at all.

It just feels like peace.

Is Ignorance Bliss?

The more I know the more I want to know.

The more I want to know the more I know that I don't know.

Get it?

I'm still working on it.

In a recently survey one of the questions was " I don't know."

The question, not the answer. Choose 1 for strongly agree to 10 strongly disagree. Even surveys are asking us about not knowing or whether we think we know or not.

Know what?

Ourselves?

Human nature?

The origins of the universe ?

The what, why, when, where, or how of anything?

So much information, often too much information everywhere.

That being said, in this day ignorance might be bliss on a multitude of levels.

The more I know the more I DON'T want to know in regards to an increasing number of issues.

We are bombarded with information.

On limitless topics.

Some topics are quite controversial, anxiety provoking and frustrating.

Some are just plain annoying and irritating.

Do we need to pick and choose what we know for peace of mind?

Is it possible?

"I don't know" is a vulnerable statement.

There are people who avoid it like the proverbial plague.

They would rather "fake it to make it" instead of admitting they don't know something.

Isn't that what "on the job training" is all about?

We have all "fudged" a few things in our careers to get ahead.

Perhaps we said in a job interview that we could type when we couldn't do any more that "hunt and peck". To appear, on Monday morning, as if we could type we feverishly pounded on a keyboard over a weekend until we mastered typing enough to do the job.

We self-administered a crash course in typing and arrived Monday morning none the wiser.

Does "I don't know" make anyone a lesser person?

Perhaps in a job interview - if the skill is crucial - but in the grand scheme of things it's not a reflection on the person.

Is most of life on a "need to know" basis?

Certainly we need to know a great deal of things to survive and thrive.

HOWEVER, when is too much information too much information?

When does the bombardment of knowing adversely affect our daily lives, and our mental, emotional and psychological health?

From my vantage point - quite often.

Media keeps us in a constant state of anxiety and information overload 24/7.

Plus, it's not the life-altering info; it's the inane, the repetitive and the down-right useless.

I find it quizzical that there is so much obsession with people we don't know, never met, worked with, dated, or have as a friend or family member.

Why, oh, why do I need to know any of this and why, oh, why is it a top news story?

Beats me.

Morbid curiosity?

I'm still doing my best to decipher how we're going to feed and clothe everyone - not just in my country, but in the world.

Then there is the proverbial blitzkrieg on social media twenty-four hours a day.

We get no relief, no respite, and have little recourse other than to turn everything off and shelter ourselves from too much information.

In the meantime, let's examine "I don't know, but I'll find out."

My take on that phrase?

Genius.

Simple.

Understated.

Elegant.

It says: "I'm secure enough to tell you I don't know and helpful enough to find out for you."

Can one possibly know everything about their job, business or position?

Can one possibly know EVERYTHING about ANYTHING?

I doubt it.

Even the smallest businesses have unexpected circumstances crop up.

There is a delicate dance between "I don't want to know", "I don't

know" and "I don't know, but I'll find out."

When is "I don't want to know" self-preservation?

When is "I don't know" vulnerability or just plain lack of information?

When is "I don't know, but I'll find out" healthy, elucidating and educational?

The answers are individual and unique.

The only answer I have to all of those questions is:

"I don't know....

...but I'll find out."

We can do our BEST to find out, even though some "I don't knows" are just not meant to be known...no matter how hard we try to get "the answer".

What Makes You YOU?

Can you tell me

what makes you you?

Is it your eyes of green
or brown
or blue?

Is it the scent you wear,

or your running shoes?

I ask again:

What makes you YOU?

Is it your brains or braun?

Hair of red,

or brown

or blonde?

Is it the funds

in your bank account,

the shape of your nose,

what you dream about?

Could it be your style,

your clothes?

Is it ANY of those?

Is it your friends

or your family?

The car that you drive,

the business you lead?

What makes you YOU?

Will we ever know?

For me, it's the love inside

it's the pain

and the growth.

Sometimes it's what we do,

sometimes what we say.

That's what makes you YOU

every single day!

When Things Don't Go As Planned.

Be prepared for things not to go as planned.

Often.

A few years ago I arrived in California to help my son move cross country to go to university.

Our trip, mode of transportation, and arrangements to move his belongings cross-country did not turn out as planned. We had to rearrange all of our plans, everything at the last minute…to arrive on time…the day before New Year's Eve.

It was a stressful time.

I needed a new cell phone…that did not go as planned.

I wanted to see my friends in one area…that did not go as planned.

The car we rented to pick up at midnight near our destination…THAT did not go as planned.

My exercise routine, my eating, my sleep… yep, you guessed it, none of it went as planned.

BUT…

In most instances it turned out for the better.

The trip ended up being safer and easier.

The cell phone could wait for two weeks and be a better deal.

I ended up seeing some very good friends and spent more time with them without being rushed.

Better than planned.

We become so attached to things working out exactly as we envision them in our minds.

We follow our list and check it off as we go. Any diversion from that list and we are thrown off.

We get disappointed, frustrated and stressed.

What the hell for? What does frustration, worry and stress do FOR us?

I'll tell you what it does for us. It damages us!

Our white blood cells start working overtime.

Our brains and hormones go into fight or flight mode, and cortisol is released at a rapid pace.

We trigger inflammation, take shallow breaths, talk too quickly, eat too quickly and make mistakes.

We lose things, break things, and forget things.

We get snippy with our loved ones and our friends.

We don't pay attention to our driving and nearly get into accidents.

OR

We get into accidents.

We overindulge to numb or self-soothe.

Not only doesn't any of that work, it backfires.

We gain weight, get wrinkles, indigestion and a craving for not-so-healthy midnight snacks.

NOW we have to reset just to get back to where we were when we started.

There are enough external pressures in our lives simply by living.

Instead of freaking out about all those things that are not going as planned I'm taking more deep breaths.

I'm taking more time out, and giving myself more attention.

I'm sitting for five minutes just to pay attention to my breath going in and out. After all, that is what the Buddha did to attain enlightenment. While I may never be enlightened, I can certainly be calmer and more at peace with myself and my surroundings.

I'm doing my best to see the bigger picture. Asking myself in the moment "is this REALLY dire?" If it is dire can I ask for help? You'd be surprised how many people, even strangers, ARE willing to help if they can.

One of the easiest ways to get out of your head, your emotions and reactions is to follow this simple meditation…you won't even realize you are meditating. I promise it works even for those who say they can't meditate.

Follow your breath, in and out of your nose.

That's it!

What could be more simple?

Just take those few moments.

It can do you a world of good when things don't go as planned.

We Shall See.

A humble monk once said to me:
"Any occurrences in life
adopt
We shall see."

My horse ran away.
How tragic, indeed,
Ah yes, no doubt,
we shall see.

My horse returned
What a joy I believe.
That may be true.
Again,
we shall see.

When you agree
we shall see
Is a gentler, peaceful
way to be;

Less disappointment,
less grief,
more relaxed,
more free.

Can it work for you?
Does it work for me?

Ah yes,
you've got it.
We shall see.

"When Something Can Go Wrong on the Road, It Might. And That's Ok

I'm writing from a hotel computer in a rather remote location.
The reason?
Early this morning a cup of coffee was accidentally spilled on my computer.
You've may have been there.
I got the kiss of death on the screen: a white folder with a black question mark in it.
What does that mean? Au revoir, trusty laptop.
It turned on for a while after I dried it with a hair dryer.
Now?
Nada. Rien. Null. Zero.
To say I'm frustrated, because most of the last fifteen years of my life personally and professionally was on that computer, is an understatement.
I hadn't backed it up to an external hard drive or the cloud for over a year.
I wasn't using it that much, except to cross reference information with my desktop and occasionally write on the road.
My mistake for not backing it up with a vengeance every week.
There are no computer stores for many, many miles from where I'm staying.
Even an authorized store trained to take a look at a computer to see if anything can be retrieved is also at least a hundred miles away.
This trip was purposefully off the beaten trail.
First, my computer was not synced with the cloud like my desktop, cellphone or tablet.
How did I overlook that? OPERATOR ERROR!
Needless to say, I'm angry, but I can't be too angry because it

was truly an accident.

THE LESSON?

Stay present, because the moment you go on autopilot things like this happen.

We start going through our day, often mindlessly executing tasks, we space out and then BAM.

When you work remotely, are on the road for business, or have a computer with memories, files, and photos in it it's essential to keep files backed up and do your best to make allowances for hiccups.

Or big, ugly burps.

Let my misfortune be your forewarning.

In addition, this doesn't mean just your computer, but anything you value that is expensive to replace or irreplaceable.

Most importantly, even on holidays and vacations, don't check out.

I love the saying from the 1936 Olympic rowing team: "Keep your mind in the boat."

The biggest lesson?

Be more conscious.

More present.

More in the moment.

More connected to yourself and your world.

"Keep your mind in the boat."

Go Beyond.

Go beyond appearances
Beyond attachments
Beyond circumstances
Beyond isolation
Beyond judgments
Beyond agendas
Beyond impressions
Beyond impositions
Beyond worry
Beyond sadness.

Go towards love
Towards acceptance
Towards compassion
Towards understanding
Towards support
Towards nurturing
Towards realization
Towards empowerment
Towards fulfillment
Towards courage

Go beyond,
towards…

Love, Compassion, Aloofness.

Full of love and compassion

but prone to play little games

with myself.

Test myself.

To be voracious one moment

and complacent the next.

To learn the hard way how to say

NO.

Age and experience has created

a mostly endearing quirkiness.

But at the same time an occasional

aloof treatment of the world

and it's shortcomings.

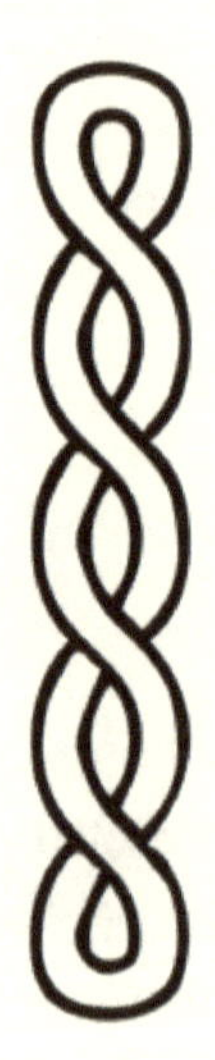

That Old Lady

As the hot water tumbled over my head and shoulders,
I stood as the water fall running from the volcanic river.
I moved and stretched.
I breathed and flowed.
Unaware of the single person audience.
But through closed eyes, I felt the stare.
I wasn't willing to immediately open my eyes.
As my movement ritual concluded, and I stepped away from the
waterfall,
a tanned and broad shouldered man approached me quizzically.
"Do you teach yoga"?
"No, I'm a Qigong and meditation teacher."
Which elicited the response of:
"I thought to myself as I watched you, man, that old lady knows
what she's doing
"Old lady?"
Old lady?
Did my ears deceive me?
Would someone be so bold or brash to compliment me and insult
me at the same time?
Were they lacking that much awareness?
Looking at me through the eyes of judgment and ignorance.
I managed to chuckle and grin through gritted teeth.
Contemplating the options of responding
"thank you"
or
"fuck you".
My actions superseded my potential words.
"Hmmm" I managed, turned on my heels and walked away.

Maturity overriding a knee-jerk response.
Sometimes the less said,
the better.

Yin Yang.

It's all in how
you look at it.
It's all Yin and Yang,
all up and down.
It's back and forth,
side to side,
yes and no,
and definitively
dark and light.
Make no mistake,
not everything
is going to meet
in the middle.
And
That's
Just
Fine.

Who Wants To Live Forever?

Who wants to live forever?
This is an interesting question posed by Queen.
Written in 1986 by Brian May for the film Highlander and
recorded by Queen with Freddie Mercury singing lead.
The Highlander, Connor McLeod, had to endure the aging and
subsequent death of his beloved wife Heather because he
himself was immortal.
The song itself became a sort of anthem for Mercury due to his
battle with AIDS.
Today it's the fifth most requested song at funerals.
Wow.
Who DOES want to live forever?
I think about it on occasion.
Wouldn't it be remarkable to see the advancements in our world
through science if we lived indefinitely?
To watch our children, grandchildren and great children grow and
mature.
To see illnesses cured and the environment healed.
Or not.
If no one died it would certainly be an even more crowded planet.
At what age would we stop aging? In our 20's, 30's, 40's, 80's?
An entire industry - the anti- aging industry would be wiped out.
Maybe even the vitamin and supplement industry.
What about hospitals, physicians and medical researchers?
No need for them if we are immortal.

BUT could we still get sick or injured and would we be relegated
to living sick and injured forever?
Trust me, I've spent a bit of time thinking about this. Probably too much.

On the other hand what if we were able to live long, healthy, extended lives, into our 100's and one day our body just gives out or we decide we are done? We feel complete.
We have accomplished goals, made contributions to the planet and our community, friends and family.
We have lived life fully and with gusto.
We have not taken for granted our time, our health, our planet or the people around us.
What if we've know exactly what we have and used that time wisely? We taught each other the value of a life well lived. A life that is not simply ego-centric.
Life lived without fear of judgment or ridicule.
We did not harm ourselves, harm others or get our good off of the backs of others.
Exercise is a pleasure and done to keep our body healthy and happy. It's a big part of who we are and not what we HAVE TO do. We incorporate it into our lives.
The planet is respected and protected because we know it has to sustain us indefinitely.
Alternatives to plastics and fossil fuels are the norm and not the exception to keep us and our world thriving.
Imagine how many diseases this behavior would eradicate.
All farmers would farm organically and use natural means to prevent pests. Then we wouldn't be putting pesticides in our bodies, water and air, therefore, preventing cancers, lung, heart and digestive diseases.
Live longer, do more.
Build more schools, homes, wells, sanitary disposal methods.
Clean drinking water for all!
The few would not need to hoard or amass untold wealth because simple pleasures would be easily attainable, respected AND appreciated.
If you knew you were going to live for 100, 200 years, or more,

would you want to live with hate, filth, and corruption knowing it was a long haul and you would have to endure those conditions for possibly centuries?

Then why do we do it now knowing our lives are relatively short? Aging is a precious gift and not everyone around us will have the luxury of aging?

Instead of being nonchalant about our lives, bodies, minds and environment we need to nurture ourselves to have the best life possible, for as long as possible.

It's possible. It's MORE than possible, it's achievable.

I hear people saying right now "but I haven't taken care of myself. I have all these problems."

There is no time like the present to turn your life around to be the best it can be RIGHT NOW.

It may not be perfect. But what is perfect? It WILL be better.

I have a picture of myself at age 2 or 3. In the picture is me, my father, my grandmother, my great-grandmother and my great, great-grandmother. 5 generations! Not many can say they have lived long enough to have a photo taken of 5 generations of their family.

My earliest family was from hearty stock. They lived at a time where some medical advances were taking hold and where life wasn't full of toxins, disposable conveniences and distractions. They also lived at a time where money and stuff wasn't the sum total of their worth.

Exercise, healthy food, a sense of community and a positive outlook were integrated into their lives. These were not elements they had to seek out, pay for, or make time for, in the course of the day. They WERE the course of the day.

Who has time to live a healthy life?

YOU DO!

We have modern conveniences to help us live simpler lives.

Pick up a bread maker, food processor or air fryer at a local thrift and consignment store. Most likely they've barely been used and are a fraction of their original costs. These machines practically do all your chopping, kneading, blending and cooking for you. Set it and forget it. The next thing you know you have healthy, no preservatives or additives bread and delicious smells wafting throughout your kitchen.

Do some of the prep on the weekends.

I'm by no means a goddess in the kitchen but with a few inexpensive and simple machines helping me prepare meals we eat a lot healthier.

Grow some herbs on your balcony, patio, or in your garden. Inexpensive and easy. A little tending and you have fresh basil in your pasta sauce. It's other worldly. Basil from a plant instead of a bottle!

Park your car farther away from the entrance to a store and get in a little walk.

Climb the stairs.

If you can't do that turn on your computer and find a chair workout. What interests you? Read about it. Can't afford a book? A library card is free and so are the books. Or spend a quarter at a library book sale.

You can hack the heck out of life to make it better.

Aging doesn't have to be a slog, and it isn't forever.

You say you were dealt a crappy hand of cards?

You may not be able to turn it into a royal flush but what about a pair. (Sorry for the Vegas metaphor.)

You get the lemons into lemonade thing, right?

There are people much worse off than any of us who are - as they say- crushing it!

If we sit feeling sorry for ourselves we rot. We disintegrate and fade from existence.

There is so much out there within our grasp to make life better. Not perfect, but better.

"Who wants to live forever?"
Forever can be lived in a day.
One beautiful day.
Time for us to live it.

Good Samaritan.

"Mommy mommy."
He cried.
My ball! My ball!
Where did it go?
He points across the street.
I can't see his ball.
"Oh my ball, my ball"
"Ok, sweetheart, hold on.
We have to be careful crossing the street. "
I don't see it.
I'm so sorry.
I can't find it.
Feeling at a loss and powerless
as traffic whizzes by.
This is not a safe search.
Even for a much loved ball.
I look under cars from across the street.
No ball.
Clutching my 3 year old's hand
I try to explain that it is gone.
Then behind me
"M'am? M'am?
Here."
This stranger opens his hand
and gives the ball to my son.
He bursts into an ear to ear grin.
I look at my son,
so relieved.
I turn to thank this Good Samaritan

but he is gone.
Gone.
I look up and down the streets.
No sign of him.
Nothing.
Not a trace.
"Where did he go?"
I look at my son and repeat:
"Where did he go?"
He shrugs his shoulders
while staring at his prized possession.
What just happened?
A kind human being
did a very good deed
with no needs for praise
then he went on his way.
All for a boy and his ball.

Thoughts For Younger Generations From Someone Who Has Been There.

Friends, I must admit it's not going to be easy.

As many triumphs as you have you will have that many setbacks and failures. You will make monumental mistakes.

You will work with people who do not have your best interest at heart. You will have jobs you love and jobs you despise.

Life will throw you curveballs that are completely unexpected.

You will choose friends who may be fair weather, betray you and take you for granted.

You will eat, drink and smoke things that in the moment are enjoyable but in the long run will do you harm.

You will take things, situations and people for granted. You may even use things, people and situations to your advantage. It will be a short-lived advantage. You will cry, you will hurt, you will be brought to your knees.

In the long run, expect the unexpected.

That all sounds pretty negative. Here is some of the "good stuff":

Embrace those people who are there for you. People you didn't realize care as much for you as they do.

The wonders of your work and the successes in your work will far outshine the failures and the challenges.

If you listen to your body it will tell you on a moment by moment basis what it needs and what it does it need. What is good for you and what isn't.

You will experience deep and profound love.

You will get what you give. When others behave with you the way you behave with them you will understand.

What you radiate, you will receive.

The hardest lessons you learn will be the best lessons you learn and will stick with you for your entire life.

Relationships, friendships and love will come and go. It's the ones that stay that need to be nurtured, maintained and supported. They will reveal themselves to you. It's important to be open enough and aware enough to see them.

Make no mistake, so much is out of your control. No person, place, or thing is in your control. You are the only person in control of you and sometimes that falters. However, this will only have to occur once or twice before you truly get it. Nothing feels better than "getting it", and you WILL get it.

You'll open your eyes one morning and be 50, 60 or 70. You'll realize that you have less time left than you've already spent. Get out of bed, get dressed and go outside. Greet every day like it's your best friend.

That being said, let go of bad friends, bad food, bad relationships, bad work, bad circumstances, and bad situations. It won't take long to decipher the good from the bad. You can do it. If you feel stuck call a reliable friend, family member, colleague or a hot line. Nothing is permanent.

Do your best to look at your life through fresh eyes every morning, afternoon and evening.

Do your best to not allow yourself to get bogged down by what's not working, what you want but are not getting, being rigid, setting yourself up for disappointment, being swayed by things that just aren't true, fact or evidence. When you allow yourself to do that, you are living your optimum life.

Allow yourself the time to realize what is the best life for you.

No one knows better. No one. It all starts with you. Give yourself the time and space to learn and grow. Be your genuine, authentic self. This is your life… no one else's.

NOW take a nice deep breath in and out and LIVE!

All Roads Lead To Where I Am Going.

I miss the exit.
I take a wrong turn
The GPS guides me down the wrong street.
But,
All in all,
All roads lead to where I'm going.
I misread the map.
I am confused by the signs.
I exit too early.
But,
All in all,
All roads lead to where I'm going.
I lose my sunglasses.
I don't bring enough change for the toll booth.
I misplace my reading glasses.
But,
All in all,
All roads lead to where I'm going.
I trust the advice.
I listen to the directions
Then I get a flat tire.
But,
All in all,
All roads lead to where I'm going.
I regain my bearings.
I remain alert
I recalculate my direction.
I trust my instincts.
I stay in the best lane.

I take the correct exit.
I apply pressure to the brakes.
I merge.
I swerve
On occasion I make a U-turn.
AND
All in all,
All roads lead to where I'm going.

NOTES